OUT OF ORDER

OUT OF
ORDER

Alexis Sears

AUTUMN
HOUSE PRESS
pittsburgh

This project is supported in part by the National Endowment for the Arts. To find out more about how National Endowment for the Arts grants impact individuals and communities, visit www.arts.gov.

Autumn House Press receives state arts funding support through a grant from the Pennsylvania Council on the Arts, a state agency funded by the Commonwealth of Pennsylvania, and the National Endowment for the Arts, a federal agency.

Cover art: Suzanne Valadon, "The Acrobat," 1916 © 2021 Artists Rights Society (ARS), New York
Text and cover design: Chiquita Babb

ISBN: 978-1-637680-32-2
Library of Congress Control Number: 2021950318

For my mother, the champion

Contents

Sky, You Don't Get It

You could place your hand in a ripe fruit and withdraw a beautiful afternoon.

—Kenneth Koch

I'm learning something every ravishing day,
and none of it is easy. I admit
my former self has drifted miles away.

I'm fortunate my loved ones seem to stay
with me (I'm sure it's rough). They never quit.
I'm learning something every ravishing day.

The sky is prettiest on sad days, way
too beautiful to understand this shit.
My former self has drifted miles away,

though sometimes it returns. It's so cliché
to have some loud internal screaming fit.
I'm learning something every ravishing day:

my lush best friend could *end* someday (we say
she'll *end* instead of die). Fed up, she'll split,
her former self drifting, drifting away,

her eyelid wings now on her back, betray
our tenderness. She won't, though. She's got grit.
I'm learning something every ravishing day
about my former self, miles away.

3

Objet d'Art

Good lives make bad stories.

—Car Seat Headrest

1.

My best friend really is a work of art—
the architecture of her vertebrae,
her bones like stilts we fear will fall apart
but don't. Inside her van, thoughts ricochet
but chocolate milkshakes thick in plastic straws
retain our silence. Women with gray hair
walk through the parking lot, talk menopause
too loudly, joke of having an affair.
My best friend cocks her brows; I check my phone.
A faceless man cries, "Please, something to eat!"
I watch her. Does she also feel alone,
or is it only me, or does the heat
explain the glossy chasm in her eye?
I want to tear apart the peach-stained sky.

2.

I want to tear apart the peach-stained sky,
my blistered fingers twitching as I shred
it into curly strips. I don't know why
I'm always like this, or what lies ahead
for girls like me. I never seem to grow
up gracefully. Example: twenty-three,
still lusting after rock stars who don't know
their sharp and track-marked arms cure my ennui
when I pace in the darkness. Can I scream,
let down my hair on starless summer nights,
paint my bored face with orange the way I dream?
Then drift through outer space on satellites?
I'll tell myself that nothing matters here,
it doesn't matter if I disappear.

3.

It doesn't matter if I disappear
the time some guy slurs, "God, you're hard to read."
I'm seventeen, untouched, morose. I hear
blue sirens, old school hip-hop, see a bead
of sweat fall from his forehead, and he smirks,
"It's seven inches, easy. Wanna take
a picture?" The real tragedy? This works
on some girls. Not asleep and not awake,
we kiss behind the frat house, in the alley,
swimming in a sea of crushed up Budweiser
cans. If this is TV, the finale
shows *me*, a girl with no one to advise her
as she drifts through smoke that smells like stale sin.
I wonder when my real life will begin.

4.

I wonder when my real life will begin.
Has it already? I'm a bloodied fist,
my knuckles peeking through the walls, my grin
stretching out in the summer. I insist
I'm happy. I am, really. Cheap Moscato,
Brie, and berries fill the fridge. I spend
afternoons downtown, eating gelato
from the creamery. The only friend
I need is in my skin, wearing my name.
I won't discuss my sadness anymore
(even in poems) or relentless shame
that once was drunk and sloppy on the floor,
convulsing. After all, *there's no more pain.*
I say this regularly to my brain.

5.

I see this regularly in my brain,
a fantasy more fascinating than most:
two clones of me in plastic lawn chairs feign
annoyance when bombarded by a host
of suitors clad in velvet jackets. This time
no men who leave without an explanation,
whose words ignite your cheeks like booze and lime:
"You're free. Don't talk to me again." Vacation
homes in Brazil and Greece. The clones will flaunt
their swimsuits. Courtney once said, "You don't need,
like, beauty. Damn. Fuck anyone you want."
Remember that. Remember I'll succeed.
I'll cruise with class, an overflowing wallet,
I'll find true love or lust, whatever you call it.

6.

I'll find true love or lust. Whatever you call it,
it kills you with its filthy melodrama!
I grab my shaky larynx, and I haul it
into the garbage, nauseous from the trauma
of being so disposable. I'm fighting
the urge to whisper platitudes, to speak
in riddles like I always do when writing.
This constant posturing is a "technique"
I'm starting to regret. It takes its toll
on you—the achy smiles, the *Believe in
fate, things happen for a reason, soul
mate* crap. What was I ever doing, even?
I should have been more honest from the start:
are any of us really works of art?

Golden Years

When Christine asks me to describe my *history of depression*,
I tell her about the Christmas video. I'm four, maybe five,
twirling a pigtail while my brother opens his toy race car.
"You looked so sad," my mother said years later.
"I didn't realize." Christine hands me a box of tissues,
and I joke that I can't believe I'm crying.
At night, I wander in dark-lit rooms while Bowie croons
through headphones. I dream of handcuffs,
of running pointy fingers through a young man's curls,
a serrated knife scraping a slope of a smile onto his flesh.
Even the sun is a philanderer, bringing home roses
to every woman on earth, its rays shading its face like a cap.

Some Days Are Harder: A Canzone

I'm slowly learning that I should adore
myself. I know I can't ever go back
to sleepless nights and angst. The word *adore*
is so poetic (Shakespeare "did adore
a twinkling star," remember?) or a rock
music trope: "It's *you* that I adore.
You'll always be my whore." But I adore
the word, the innocence. I think it's right
to be naïve and vulnerable, to write
yourself a villanelle or maybe eight (or
more). It's for the aching soul, you see:
it's like Camembert, like lounging by the sea.

I don't know if anyone will see
the point in arrogance, this whole "adore
myself" thing. Cocky with a massive *C*.
I think my brother might. I sometimes see
him in my own reflection, in the back
on bus rides, even though it's pretty easy
to know he's far away, at least, to see
the harbor in his photos, or the Hard Rock
Cafe downtown, the place where (our Barack
condemned them) riots happened. Can't I see
that all the world's in pain? I see it right
there on the news. My mother says, "All right,

enough. You need some sleep, or maybe write
all afternoon, or drive down to the sea,
until you realize that you'll be all right
again." I spend the evenings in the bright
light that simulates the sun, a door
to my apartment open. Is it right
to eavesdrop on my neighbor even right

before he kicks the bucket? He's gone back
to hacking in the mornings, even back
to crying, so I've heard. I used to write
about whether he'll die in style, rock
a silver necklace or a massive rock,

the band tight on his finger. Does it rock
to be old? Doubt it. Think about James Wright:
"I've wasted my life." Yikes. "A total crock
of bullshit," Caitlyn said once at a rock
concert—no, a restaurant, fricassee
in bowls before us, the potatoes rock-
hard. "My friend from UC Irvine, Brock,
hates that poem, too. God, I adore
him." I know Caitlyn always adores
pretention, like that sculptor who carved rocks
but seemed to think he ruled the country, back
when we all thought we'd end up happy, back

then. I tell myself not to go back
to constant reminiscing. "Never rock
the boat," I tell myself, "by thinking back
to everyone who screwed you over." Back
to basics: deep breaths, pasta. Of course, writ-
ing. Maybe a tat across my back:
I heard the news today (not *Don't look back
in anger*). Why get a tat you can't see,
though? So why not something I *can* see?
On my shoulder, maybe. In the back
of my own conscience, I know I'd adore
a floral one that tells me to "adore

myself." Yes, I remember. I'd adore
myself if I were edgy. I don't see
the point of anything these days. Why rock
a smile if it's not authentic, right?
Mine once was. Yours, too. Wanna go back?

The Wedding Gown

With a line from Chidiock Tichborne

My coworker's face twists like a cubist painting
when I tell him I found my wedding dress, tainting
his spotless afternoon. Clearly, he's equating

my honesty with crazy—*What the fuck?*—slamming
his Corona, his fingers limp and icy, on the table. The damn thing—
the wedding dress, I mean—has never gotten this reaction. Jamming

the lime back in the bottle's tiny open mouth, he goes quiet.
I do, too. Maybe I should keep this one a secret. *My* shit-
show of a love life, after all, that doesn't lend itself to marriage, is a riot

(my college roommate called my life "a sitcom"). Obsession
is my mother tongue: the indie drummer who pounds his aggression
to a powder, the blisters on his hands ornaments, the singer's lyrics of
   depression

now irrelevant; three pages of a spicy sonnet crown,
each iamb sizzling, onions in a pan; my eyes in certain pictures, brown
as light roast coffee beans in filters; boots that make my ankles bleed. And
   now, the gown,

its long sleeves lacy, suited for a goddess; a tease of a neckline; a tulle,
pearl skirt that falls like freshly straightened hair. My best friend texts me,
   "Cool.
I like the bodice" when I send her yet another picture. "You know, the
   golden rule,"

she says. "Stop looking for love. That's when it arrives."
But one by one, as classmates turn to brides, I wonder if their new domestic
   lives
have meaning more than mine, and if this whole "obsession" thing survives.

Does it just sail away? Or is it killed too suddenly to suffer, a victim
of a palm tree through a windshield? I want to sneer and even contradict
    him
when my coworker mumbles *so bizarre.* Or turn to friends and laugh, "See
    how I tricked him!"

and he'll relent. The jackass knows I've won.
But what's the point of speaking now? It's done.
My glass is full, and now my glass is run.

Luck

I was a kid. I didn't hear
the gunshot, didn't dip my fingers
in the blood. Only a phone call, Mom
on a moss-colored sofa, my brother's
freckled eyes, aging. I was lucky,
my therapist said: *You didn't find the body.*
Your father protected you from that. Finding
that missing sock, a wrinkle-free twenty on
concrete—luck is funny, isn't it? My luck
comes from the sea, which my father had
crossed years before, miles away when he died,
when he lived. Some days I grieve what I had,
some days I grieve what I didn't, more haunted
by the choppy shots of him—close-ups of his silver car,
his teeth—than the shot I can only imagine.

What Is History?

It wasn't until after his death that I thought
about my father's complexion. He was dark,
like an avocado pit or kiwi skin or the inside
of a pecan pie. Nothing like mine, a caramel cliché,
"not black," the white boys on the school bus taunted, lips
coated in spit. At fifteen, I sat cross-legged
on a Persian rug watching BET, mouthing along
with Dave Chapelle, fixating on the figure-eight swivels
of mile-wide hips in rap videos. Black power fists
in AP US History, devouring Malcolm and Jesse
Jackson. Dad, would you have told me what to say
when the syrup-skinned girls at the Black Student Union
asked "What are you?" and "Why are you here?" And do you think
I have the right to grieve—what am I grieving anyway?—
when you're gone and everything has changed, except
nothing's changed? But this isn't about you, not about how
even now, you watch me while I watch TV, watching black
boys choke and bleed while the ceiling fan watches, face-down.

Skin

The canyons are rough like the skin
on our elbows. We wash our plates

in the river, lie on our backs with our nails in the sand.
He is not a Renaissance statue;

he's a hipster-chic art student's favorite sculpture, arms

made of clay, pennies for eyes.
I watch him take off his dirty T-shirt,

the sweat on his forehead dripping onto his lashes,
his shoulder blades sunburnt and sharp.

The girls where I'm from don't look like you.
Rhode Island is like vanilla bean ice cream. No color.

We talk about Ayn Rand and Adderall, SAT prep,
the morning he cried in a beat-up red Ford after

hunting with his father.
He says, *"Stairway to Heaven" is a cheesy nightmare,*

tells me how junior year, the damn song played as he fumbled
for a condom, hands shaking as he reached to feel
the cheerleader's freckled chest,

reached to feel anything.

I don't know if I've ever loved anyone, he shrugs. *Have you?*

I don't count the blond hairs on his chin
or the cracks in his trembling voice.
I close my eyes, and we're in a kitchen

with bright yellow walls, swing dancing
to Bowie and The Strokes while the biscuits burn,

hard like the boulders beside us, black as the rapids below.

Hermosa Beach

The final scene: I'm with my best friend. We're at a bar on the boardwalk,
    margaritas in hand while the ocean runs over the rocks like blood on bony kneecaps.
        I want to go home. I want to cocoon myself in comforters, read Henry James,

get drunk off the Moscato I paid for in quarters. In hazy groups, the clouds turn in
    for the night, growing sleepy and bored while men in swim trunks, their hair golden
        gossamer, talk football. A woman, disrobing the Snickers from her purse, slurs,

"Bono's mom died when he was, like, fourteen. Sad, right?" A saucer-eyed girl squashes a cigarette
    beneath a dirty white shoe before lighting up another. I'm afraid to meet anyone's gaze.
        Tonight, I'll be afraid to dream. I've become a drawing in the dark, my skin

ashy and blurred, fingers running along the edge of the table. I don't need to be seen.
    What I need is a second chance, to learn to build pyramids with my laugh alone,
        to bathe in the craters of the moon. Soon, the bar closes. Soon, we'll be gone.

At the New Year

Yet again—I won't admit how many
times I've done it—I'm kilometers
away from seashore, drifting with the current
of my sixth-grade yearbook, sifting through
the sloppy seaweed spelling out, *You rock!*
and *Have an awesome summer!* As addictions
go, I think it's pretty weak. Why not
group sex like the rock musicians, or
crystal meth like Joe from Chevron? I've
gone home now for the winter, my blue room
a whirlwind of destruction, those debate
team trophies jammed beneath the bed where some
dumb nights I dream about a boy I thought
I loved—or was it someone else? My one-
time best friend, six three, connoisseur of beer,
his bald spot quarter-sized and slowly growing?—
the two of us slow-dancing on a pitcher's
mound in outer space with Nutter Butter
crumbs stuck in our braces (neon green).
But now I'm older, and those shaky hands
are phantom pressures on my waist. Today
the sky is like a schmear—thick, creamy pink—
and on my laptop, Flea plucks at his bass
while sweat drips from his off-white, hairless chest.
I don't know why I'm like this still. A text.
A Hallmark card. A Facebook post. It's all
collected here and echoing. When we
were young, my one-time best friend looked at me
and asked if I could ever fall in love
with him someday. I smirked and answered "Nope."

Intimacy

I.

In my favorite Bollywood movie that I watch with a friend from New Delhi,
a man tells his friend: *Girls like you aren't made for flirting. They're made for love.*

My friend, her hair like spilled black paint,
placed a hand over her chest, blushing as the Dallas heat

poured through the window, our dinner plates glistening
discs. This was before we blew hookah smoke

into each other's mouths, our lips barely grazing each other's
until they inevitably joined, and our drunken tongues

and hungry arms entwined. This was before I gathered
all my coats and pushed my tattered boxes across the lobby of our dorm.

II.

Someone in Manhattan Beach sits hunched over his piano
playing Elton John, his fingers

leaving fossils in the keys. By now, everyone has died:
Bowie, Prince, and Chuck dance beside Amy, Freddie, Jim, Kurt.

A barista rolls her eyes at me: "How can you cry over random
guitar junkies you didn't know? Were you and Kurt Cobain even alive

at the same time?" Then, "Classic white girl." It's true:
I cry in Priuses, in bedrooms, in my poems. I tell myself to smile,

even as the wide sky turns to steel. Or when I see my mother sleep alone.
When my teenage brother says, "I'm going to get a tattoo of my dick

on my dick," I don't burst into tears when I picture dick tattoos
in an infinite regress. In school, young men are taught to fuck the Earth.

III.

In the sestina (Ashbery's "The Painter," for example), the final envoy
contains all six end words, two per line, placed in the middle.

Formal poetry makes me feel safe and sane. Perhaps that's why I stopped
writing it. "Do you think you're Milton?" a professor asks me endearingly

as snow collects outside. I admire his candor, his fluidity, his scarf.
I want to wrap us both in down, to sip Sleepytime tea from golden mugs

so we can doze through the flames after we light ourselves on fire,
our every waking thought turning to ash. Once, in Maryland,

I saw a man so beautiful I burst into tears and tried to rip
my skin off. (People have always been surprised by that.)

Does that matter? I don't think it really matters.
It was very long ago.

On Turning Twenty

There are those who suffer in plain sight.

—Randall Mann

One afternoon, my father chose to die.
He was like, *See ya later, guys.* I think
I understand, since I don't know if I

can hang, myself. But hang myself? (*Don't try,*
they whisper, spooked.) Too young to buy a drink,
but old enough to snatch one from a guy

who says, "I'm married, but—" His twinkling eye
is trained, you know, to tell me with a wink
I've made the cut. One hand explores my thigh,

the other fingering a Miller. Why
are men so callous? Nowadays, I sink
beneath the comforter. I'll never cry

because my lover's lover's lovely—Thai,
with toned and skinny limbs, her cheekbones pink
and angular. Ohio girl, a Buckeye.

I'm from a land where bleach blond angels fly.
Beneath the moonlight, friends and I will clink
our cups; my wondrous-child eyes defy
adulthood, till I sip. It's bitter, dry.

II

For My Father: A Sonnet Redoublé

1.

If you were here, you'd know how I believe
in signs. No, not astrology, but *signs*:
the dream a sexy drummer smirks, declines
my tired flirtations while I play naïve,
and stand, busty with purple lipstick, pining.
The biker gang I almost hit but dodged,
and Robin's epic nineties speech still lodged
too comfortably inside my psyche (dining
beside my other thoughts): *It's not your fault.*
You might not know, but I write poems now,
and read, while bathing, Rilke, Salter, Howe,
and Jericho, decaying minds like Walt.
Today's book starts *Dear Father.* Yes, it's true.
So, Dad, this crown of sonnets is for you.

2.

So, Dad—a crown, these sonnets, all for you.
For *me*, some time to tell you what you've missed.
I can't. I don't do much these days, subsist
on vices: doing things I shouldn't do,
like eating chips or eyeing photographs
of me, the same ones always, as I try
to spy a crumb of beauty. I apply
my makeup poorly. Still, I have to laugh
and wonder: Do we choose our flaws or vice
versa? Well, I walk outside and feel
a worldwide ache, but life's a blooper reel
for me (self-deprecating humor's twice
as fun). Be proud. Your "praise" was always spotty.
I'm learning everything you never taught me.

3.

I'm learning *everything.* You never taught me
anything, really, so I teach myself.
I find your obit—no, not on a shelf
but on the internet, eyes sore and draughty
in their sockets, this comment: "I've heard Tom
could travel across Route 50 with a blindfold
and still track down a disco." Copy, bold
it on a Word doc. Legacy.com
is now my autumn reading. I don't mind,
really. Even writing this is strange.
Pretend you'd lived. Would you try to estrange
yourself? Would I have responded in kind?
You know, I understand your thick disdain.
I'd say that overall, I'm pretty plain.

4.

"I'd say that overall, I'm pretty plain,"
I tell the man too close to me in line
at Starbucks when he says I'm *gorgeous.* Crying:
not something I do in public (brain
shrinkage caused by my depression's not
my favorite topic). Now I play forgetful.
Of course, I should have thanked him. Why regretful,
though, years later? Old news. I'll allot
an hour or so a day for self-obsession,
and then run thirteen miles, play some Mozart.
Dad, I've fooled the crowd. They think I'm "so smart,"
but this letter has become a therapy session!
(Send me a bill.) The brooding's *so* on brand.
Maybe next life, we'll hold a better hand.

5.

Maybe next life. Will holds my hand far better
than anyone. He says, "You can't be sad. Cool
girls like you are fine." I'm now in grad school,
rocking Levi's jackets, Eddie Vedder
hoodies, J. Crew sweaters, cluelessness.
God, so little experience. My friends
are baseball cards men swap for "perfect tens."
They say, "*That guy*? He used me, too." This mess
is like a different dialect to me
until it isn't. I go to a psychic
with Jen (you never met her. I'm her sidekick.)
She, purple-haired, says "Baby, only three
more awful dates until you find the one.
When *feelings* last, some deeds can't be undone."

6.

When feelings last, some deeds can't be undone—
but that's the *last* thing girls should talk about
with their own fathers! Nope, without a doubt.
It's Tuesday, and another cop, his gun
in tow, has done his part to cleanse the Earth
of color. Protests. Plague. Paralysis.
At this point, some psychoanalysis
would do me good, a spiritual rebirth.
A man, seventy-nine, I love perennially,
says, "We *must* solve the crisis—in this country—
of mental health." Kardashians. Kris Humphries.
Shootings. Instagram. Some new "millennial" we
toss aside for a busy year or ten.
Until we hear one took his life again.

7.

Until we heard you took your life . . . again,
Dad, things used to be one way and now,
I just don't know. Sometimes, I don't allow
myself to know. You only knew me when
Karl, the boy I sat behind in math,
asked, snarling, "Do you always have to say
your opinion about *everything*?" Today
(and other days), I haven't thought. The aftermath
of losing you? It's possible, unless
a mind in beige often devoid of art
was fated. We've spent thirteen years apart,
and still it's *you* I'm trying to impress.
Did you like poems, drink them by the liter?
You could have been a stan for rhyme and meter.

8.

You could have been a stan for rhyme and meter—
do you know what "stan" means? It didn't show
in the dictionary till three years ago.
A stan: a zealous fan. An overeater
of fresh red velvet cupcakes, for example,
"stans" sugar hard. And here I am, your kid,
stanning ghazals, sonnets, couplets. I'd
say that most, I stan my rock stars, trample
other stans to death inside the mosh pit
(I wish!) at concerts where I purchase fruit
for the guitarist ("ugly but so cute,"
my friend calls him. "You, sis, are an *it
girl.*" I smile, my nervousness apparent).
I know I'll make a brilliant, tragic parent.

9.

I know I'll make a brilliant, tragic parent.
Now that's my destiny. I'll run my hands
through curls (I hope they're curls!), twist every strand.
My kids—damn cultured (*Rent, Le Juif errant,*
and Dostoevsky, Plath)—are mortified
when I say to the waitress, "I can't eat
an entire *case -a- dilla*! Just one!" (*Neat
joke,* I'll tell myself. *A bona fide
comedienne here.*) When I was a child,
I read that those who lose our parents young
feel . . . what's the word used? *Other.* I'm among
the *others.* Wow. By now, I've reconciled
my *otherness* with sentiments of *sameness.*
Lately, I've found myself completely blameless.

10.

Lately, I've found myself. Completely blameless,
a girl I haven't spoken to since age
twelve sees you smiling on my Facebook page
and says, "You make him so proud." Her surname is
not what it once was. I'm jealous. *Bride*
is the title I want most. But still, I think
I can make progress. Mom asks, with a wink,
if I make *myself* proud. It echoes. *Pride:*
the truth is *proud* (like *lonely*) I can't say
it ever really occurred to me to be.
Even in secret fantasies, *carefree*
is something I can't grasp, pricey bouquet
of troubles. Soon, another will arrive,
a new arrangement destined to survive.

11.

A new arrangement: *destiny* survives,
and *fate* and *soul mates.* I'll apologize
for my skepticism, sleep, arise
perfectly rested, be that girl who thrives
beneath the pressure. Sure, astrology.
And crystals, too. Why not? The whole nine yards.
Dad, did you ever peek at tarot cards?
Were you more into demonology,
or sports, or cars, or old-school films? I guess
I'm asking, what kept you with us for as long
as you were here? God, people say I'm *strong*
as if I have a choice. But fine, I'll dress
in silky scarves, eat tacos a la carte.
Until the end, I'll keep playing the part.

12.

Until the end, I'll keep playing. The part
where our heroine gets her big break
(a music number! She'll wear a red wig, fake
lashes!) makes us cry 'cause from the start,
we *knew* she had the courage in her! Beaming,
she dances on the table in a boa.
The boys on mopeds cruising Figueroa
didn't see the movie, yet keep dreaming
of her in tights for seven weeks, at least.
I've never been a film buff, Dad, but I
spend Sundays fantasizing about pie
and *that girl*. Other characters—the priest,
the bully, moon-crossed love interest, the gun-
man, don't matter. It's *our girl* who won.

13.

Man, no matter who's our girl, who won,
what winning even is . . . it's time to wrap
this letter up. Farewell! Goodbye, ol' chap!
I'm only joking, but we may be done
here. After all, I'm running out of rhymes,
the meter's fucked, I don't have many stories.
Your brother poured your ashes on the shore (freez-
ing yourself? That's something folks in primes
of their lives do, so no, not your style).
A girl I know (she's miles away and stunning)
said I should write this. It's better than running
or boring dinners with that Francophile,
so yes, I wrote to you all afternoon!
Perhaps I'll see you someday, maybe soon.

14.

Perhaps I'll see you someday, maybe soon,
is not a solid way to end a note
to anyone, much less your father. Quote
me on that one. Just trust me. Rooms are strewn
with Lay's bags (which we already discussed),
and bottles of psychiatric meds run dry,
the eyeliner I'm learning to apply
with such finesse, a clock that needs adjust-
ing, desperately. But do you need to know
what my new bedroom looks like, or my house,
or even what I look like, how I douse
myself in face wash, if it makes me glow?
For either of us, would it be reprieve
if you were here? You know what I believe.

15.

If you were here, you'd know what I believe,
Dad: a crown of sonnets, all for you.
I'm learning *everything* ("You never taught me,"
I'd say.) Overall, I'm pretty plain,
but maybe next life, we'll have better hands
and feelings. Last, some deeds can't be undone,
and then we heard you took your life. Again,
you could have been a stan for rhyme and meter,
and watched me make a brilliant, tragic parent!
Lately, I've found myself completely blameless
in my new arrangement, destined to survive
until the end. I'll keep playing the part,
man, no matter. Who's our girl? Who won?
(Perhaps I?) See you! *Someday* may be *soon.*

Hoop Earrings, Bare Legs

I dread it, getting old, but nowadays
it's less frightening than usual. I try
acceptance, even comfort. There *are* ways

to cope. So I go to the dog park, lie
on biting blades of grass, young mothers' wrists
slick, broken out in hives. Barely July

and more humid than ever. Kids do twists
two feet above their skateboards. Three tattoos
of skeletons on hairy calves. *The trysts*

we had when we were young, a woman, booze
in a canteen beside her, laughs. And me?
I'm with four ladies over sixty, shmooz-

ing, nothing in common, we agree,
except our dogs and womanhood. I ask
myself: How did this kinship come to be?

Should I instead go shopping? Sleep? Or bask
in short pajamas, lounging in the sun?
I mean, I know that any household task

would pass the time. But *this,* this is the "fun
outing" I look forward to. There's peace
in knowing that I'm not the only one

who's sat reclined, her fingers doused in grease,
practically shoulder-deep inside a bag
of jalapeño Lay's, beneath a fleece,

comforter. Who's had to walk zigzag
between apartments trying to avoid
the men who follow, holler. The "red flag"

(or multiple) on dates. Middle-aged, Freud-
worshipping shrinks who say, "I can't relate.
I met my man when I was nineteen," void

of any sort of empathy. The weight
of foreign arms around our waists. I'm not
the only woman haunted by the state

of silence when a, frankly, smokin' hot
girl at the nightclub wearing double-digit
sizes, dabs her eyes amidst cheap shots

that catapult from strangers' mouths. They fidget
with leather wallets, quip, "See? Every girl group
has a *fat* one." What was her name? Bridget?

Jane? I wish I'd asked, taken a hoop
from my pierced ear and placed it in her palm.
I wish I'd said a goddamn thing. I stoop

when I remember it. Strawberry balm
(for lips) we pass among us, reaches broad
as cityscapes. Our *firsts.* Casual "bombs"

about our fucked-up families, dreams of Rod
Stewart in the seventies. But there
is still so little that I know of God

or sex or death, how my bare legs compare
to those of other girls my age. I want
to ask, beneath the sun's relentless glare,

if shame remains not anything we flaunt
but rather, like a tired, passé rifle
we aim at our own lace-clad breastbones, taunt,

"you're not quite good enough like *her*." I stifle
a stutter, an odd question that would kill
the mood. In Ray-Ban shades, I catch an eyeful

of Ruth, beside me, eighty-five. She's still,
serene, her veins like threads around her neck.
When does it stop? What's *it?* Waiting until

the sun goes down and others leave, I check
that she's alive. I can't explain just how
alive she is. Someday, I'll have a speck

of what *she* has. It's quiet, breezy now.
Two redheads, maybe fifth grade, eyes aglow,
toss kites into their sports car trunk and vow

that they'll behave for ice cream. There is no
more bread left over, so ducks bid farewell,
returning to their ponds. "What's next?" asks Jo.

"Drinking *again?*" "Oh, lady, go to hell!"
Ruth answers. We all laugh. A bizarre new cluster
of mismatched stars, we gather. I can smell

the newborn darkness, think about the luster
we women sometimes realize we possess
and sometimes don't. I take my shades off, muster

a goodbye, and as I walk home, my dress
grass-stained and wrinkled, I decide to think
about the bassline of my thighs, the mess

of chipping toenail polish, months-old, pink,
the sweet crescendo of my waist, the way
my curls bounce as I cross the street. I drink

in soothing nighttime air. Maybe, one day,
when I am also older, friends have died,
I'll stop giving a fuck—my tousled, gray

hair tied—about what doesn't matter, stride
in admiration of life's beauty. Streetlights.
Leaves. My key. I'm home. I go inside.

Ted Bundy

I.

The average person walks past thirty-six
murderers, I've heard, throughout a lifetime.
"They're no longer in vogue," I say to Max,
"serial killers. Now it's all mass shootings."
As if it's all the same. I look at Max.
He has the same blue eyes as my ex, Blake—
well, not my ex. Blake made it clear that I
would *never* be his girlfriend, was too jaded
from *his* ex, who "stopped taking her damn pill
and trapped" him "for attention." Once, he drank
hot chocolate while I sipped my coffee black,
and told me that if I made him upset,
"Well, let's just say I won't let that shit simmer."

II.

In the new film, an actor, who one time
was every teen girl's fantasy, plays Ted.
Indignant protestors are up in arms:
"You can't pick someone that attractive to
play one of the most heinous men of all
time!" I see their point, I guess, but don't
they know that sometimes villainous and sexy
intertwine? After he throws his hatchet
into the trunk, stepping over the woman's
body, fake blood soaks into her hair
like a cheap dye job. The audience gets
a glimpse of his protruding biceps, his
brows, perfectly coiffed, curving like lime
wedges. I cover my mouth to hide
my smile, lock eyes with the girl beside
me, who does the same, both of us giggling
at the peculiarity, or because
it's easier to laugh than sit in shame.

III.

Blake's the only man I've ever slept with,
and sometimes, when I lie in bed alone,
I think about the way he'd wrap his hands
around my throat and squeeze. I didn't know
if this was normal. He never once asked
for my permission. He'd turn on Pink Floyd
and kiss me till my bottom lip was bleeding.
Even now, I don't understand sex,
the way women in pornos scream their guts out,
surreal, and then the camera shuts off. But
afterward, Blake would pour me a glass
of water, kiss my cheek, tell me how heavenly
it was to lie beside me, and I knew
that I was safe with him, and how could I
be childish and dumb enough to doubt that?

IV.

Ted Bundy's girl, Elizabeth, knows better,
although she never dares to tell a soul.
In almost every scene, she has a bottle
in her small hands, pressed up against her lips.
She cries, ignores her daughter's wails, writes
love letters to her man behind steel bars.
She knows better, and I knew better, too.
It's almost like I'm watching my own self
on screen. I want to grab her by her shoulders,
shake her, watch her head snap back and forth,
wipe away her tears with satin while
her friend pleads, "What is it about this guy?"

V.

I haven't talked to Blake in half a year,
but truly, I don't wish him ill at all.
In fact, I sometimes picture those sweet eyes,
that smile. Liz (Ted Bundy's girl, remember?)
got sober, took her daughter, went away,
and wrote a book about the whole ordeal.
I spend my time going for walks with Max,
and though I don't believe, not necessarily,
that women have to suffer for epiphanies,
I wonder why, if I value my life,
I got involved with someone who could hurt me,
who probably would not think twice about it.
Maybe I figured I'm too sweet to harm,
that I'm far better than those other girls.
Maybe I was afraid that if I ran,
he'd kill me after all—he cared that much.
Maybe I thought this was what I deserved.

Sandwich Shop Sonnet

The *sandwich artist* at the hoagie shop—
a chubby "cool aunt" type with lime-green hair—
asks me, "Do you have a man?" I stop
and think. Should I make up a love affair?
I'll brag about my grungy Boston dude
whose Smashing Pumpkins T-shirt hides his tats;
the architect with Mensa aptitude
(he used to chair the College Democrats).
An athlete, maybe! Six-foot-three and ripped,
who tutors prisoners on his free days.
I'll find a writer type whose brilliant script
lights up my face and cures my deep malaise.
But I say, "No," my eyes fixed on my feet.
She sighs, "Here. Have this ham and swiss. My treat."

Children of the Streets

I didn't know what love was before you were born,
my mother said one night. I repeat this like a lullaby
in the shower, at the pharmacy, when my best friend
tells me—her voice slow and mechanical—that she tried
to overdose on our high school tennis court. She's nonchalant
about it, dropping it into the conversation like parsley

on a dinner plate, then sailing toward talk of sorority formals
and old-school hip-hop. I respect that. She has a Lolita vibe:
diaphanous lashes, braces even, hockey-stick legs beneath
a leopard-print slip dress. It makes people uneasy. You know,
as I walk down East Pratt Street, I usually feel like a child
myself: shoelaces tangled, my gaze unassuming,
trying to decide where I should cross,
trying to decide where I should turn.

What You've Heard

When a friend of mine forced himself on me
in a cozy bar in Federal Hill,
the flush-faced men at the next table
applauded. *Give it to her!*

I sat doll-like and open-mouthed
as my skin unraveled, my friend peeling it off
layer by layer—casually—as if I were a roll
of paper towels in the kitchen of his dorm.

At work I make calls all day, asking myself
when I became so nervous, so easy to dispose of.
Would you be willing to make a donation today for $141??
They hang up. I'm hung up on the way my mother's voice
sounds just like mine, how people get us mixed up
on the phone. I don't know why this scares me.

The key is to walk with conviction,
like you know where you're going.
I don't have to tell you that, do I?
You've heard it before.

Seven

"So tell me: on a scale of one to ten,
what would you rate your life?" Somehow, again,
I've found myself inside a stranded bar
with made-up drag queens, doughy bankers. Far

away, the girls I came with flirt with men
in navy cargo pants and boat shoes. When
was that in fashion? I'm all set to leave,
depart in silence, pizza my reprieve,

until the strange man corners me and chirps,
"What would you rate your life?" Long-nailed, he slurps
what could be one of those Long Islands, though
I just don't care. Probably, years ago,

I'd beam, but now, I want to take a knife,
and twist it into his perfect dimple. Life?
A rating system? No "hello," not even
a cheeky wink? But I choke out, "uh . . . seven?"

His mouth falls open, slug-like eyebrows raised,
"A pretty girl? Just seven? I'm amazed!
I'd give my own a nine. Thirty-two years,
near perfect." Girls behind me clink their beers,

engage in bored, half-hearted conversation,
skewered shrimp abound, the pink crustacean
I envy. Yes, I'd rather jab a stick
through me than talk to this simple-minded dick.

He presses on, "Look, I'll be honest, I—
I think it's rather sad you'd classify

your life so low. I mean, how old are you?
Too young to be so jaded!" Cheese fondue;

tiny cocktail dresses; toothpicks; just
me. He looks at me not with disgust
but hardly warmth, intrigue, or lust. I picture
pizza men, my couch. I'd skip this lecture

in some other sweet world, but now I'm stuck.
"Seven's fine," I say. "It's passing." Fuck,
I want this to be over. "Yeah, I guess,"
he snorts, "But don't you ever, like, obsess

about how things *could* be? Why settle? Fake
it till you make it! I think you should make
better decisions and you'll find the world
isn't so bad." Later, I'll wish I'd twirled

and stomped away, or kneed him in the gut,
used Mom's kickboxing skills—jab, uppercut—
blinded the cocky sucker. How *dare* he?
A stuck-up bastard whose reality

was some sick fantasy. Clearly, he never
had gone through any hardship whatsoever.
Better decisions? Really? I'd decided
to be so young and old at once, divided

into fifteen equally punctured parts?
Yes, when I got my master of fine arts,
I chose to lie face-down all day. A child,
I simply checked a box—cross-legged, and smiled—

that said I wanted my old man to die.
My God, who is this freakish, dimpled guy?
But reader, you and I both know the facts:
I'm the kind of girl who never quite reacts,

the kind whom others pity for attracting
guys who . . . who what? Love their own lives? Love acting
superior? Later, I'll wish I'd said,
well, anything, but it fills me with dread

to even dream about making a scene.
So I just laugh. "Yeah, I see what you mean.
Nice meeting you!" and hope to leave composed.
By now, I know the pizza place is closed.

Riding Home, Five Years Later

I'm a high school senior and my brother,
age sixteen, drives us home in our black Prius,
his eyes half-closed like clam shells, while his hands
narrowly graze the wheel. Turning left,
he's almost catatonic in his post-
exercise stupor. Neither of us speaks.
Occasionally, he tugs at his shirt
that reads "Peninsula High School Baseball," sweaty
and clinging to his chest. A nineties hit
blares from the stereo, a song I've always
dodged. Sometimes, the trumpets make me cry.
Hey, Chris? I ask him. *Do you ever miss
our dad? I've been thinking about it, and
I get so sad.* He squints. I picture them

in Dad's apartment, gnawing frozen waffles
and undercooked potatoes. Late night hoops
on Peck Park's basketball court. I look at my
young brother, wonder how he can be so
strong, yet in this moment, microscopic.
Silence. Then he stammers, *Do you want
a chocolate malt? I'll buy you one.* I shake
my head, feel myself parting from my body.
The car gets smaller and smaller till it's gone.

Donuts

I wonder if my roommate knows I steal handfuls of her Craisins at night; hunger is forever my favorite virtue. A nosegay of little dried fruits. These days, I no longer fight hunger.

"You want me," a boy—flannel-clad, his face darksome—taunts. Paint falls like overripe peaches off my kitchen walls. I snicker; I can't fight a man's ego, his appetite, hunger.

In a donut shop on East Mifflin Street, a girl in a leotard asks her father for both a chocolate and a glazed. He scoffs, "Two donuts—that's what you need." She looks down, ignores the slight hunger.

My best friend says, "Every time, you face-plant into these horrible relationships." Her earlobes are almost like raindrops, her voice a fresh-opened Sunkist, a woman to invite hunger.

My great-grandmother used to say, "Alexis is a special one!" Sucking on a chocolate-covered cherry, beaming and effervescent, she'd turn to me. "So polite! Hungry?"

September

I know I could do better.
I could go outside, get some sun. Instead,
I watch from my window as the snow falls
as if God is grating parmesan
over the city: *Say when.* I've never
had the chance to love desperately,
but I've felt rage worm its way through
my stomach like a parasite. So many things
I cannot say aloud: *It would be wrong to bring*
a child into the world to watch me suffer, to suffer
with me won't win me any friends.
Am I worse off than anyone else,
though? I sip my dark roast, spell my
name in carrots on the counter. I am
no longer, at least, a monument
to damage: my ribcage a coliseum,
its broken edges jabbing
at the sky. The faint sounds
of Earth, Wind & Fire play
in my kitchen, and I smile,
even shimmy a little. None of us
will last forever. Someday,
maybe soon, everything will ache
a little less.

Memory: We're Out of Limes

Vomiting into the vase on the bedside table, an adult cartoon in the background. Kevin and Caroline were there. Fluorescent lights. My too-short skirt. Him forcing himself on me while the men applauded. Hookah. A guy in leather handing me his baseball cap: "Take it, it's yours now." I remember tequila and lemon because the bar was out of limes. "Come back to my place." "Is she even conscious?" "Ma'am, you can't sleep in this establishment." I don't even remember who said what. Everything is out of order. I don't remember what happened first, how the night ended or how it started.

IV

Hair Sestina

I'm twenty-four and yes, by now I know
I have a problem. "Oh, but don't we all?"
everyone jokes as if it's really brilliant.
But not like this. A slippery chunk of life
has slid on by, and still I am without
an inkling of real knowledge about black

hairstyles. Some bus driver says, "You're 'black'
in name, but you will never *really* know
their struggles." *Their.* It sticks. I'm left without
a comeback (since I know it's true). She's all
proud now and continues on, "Your life
seems easier than most." Gee, *that* is brilliant.

I'm not sure if I'm hurt or not. A brilliant
professor told me once (her hair dyed black
as licorice bites), "Sometimes, you know, in life,
you'll want to cry but can't. Just so you know,
the answer is to bite your thumb. That's all."
My cluelessness, though? Soon, I'll be without

a thumb, a life, a man to dine with. (Out
of time.) I only care about hair now. Brilliant
black scholar is what I aim for. I spend all
my leisure time these days researching *black
hair looks.* I nod, I practice, hope I'll know
a twist-out when I see it. I watch *Life*

(the one with Eddie Murphy), plan a life
where someday I'll have cornrows, braids, without
the insecurity. Should I—oh no,
no flashcards. What's the point of being brilliant

when I wear white girl hair to Sam's Club, lack
inheritance and understanding? All

I know is this: it wouldn't be right to call
what happened to me *abandonment.* See, life
can be too hard for us, including my black
father, once-Marine, six two, without
someone to speak to, even me. Not brilliant,
but he could have helped me come to know

my hair, my blackness, self. Oh, well. Without
some emptiness, what's life? Twenty-four. "Brilliant."
"Accomplished." All I know is what I don't.

My Hair: An Epic

Part 1: The Tween Years

It never knew how to behave, a problem
child long before I was. Whatever
I begged of it, it did the opposite,
a stubborn bitch. Exhausted mother never

knew what the hell to do about it, either,
and watched on helplessly while it inflated,
crackled. Twelve years old, I was dubbed "Frizzy-
Haired Freak" while giggling friends of mine were rated

eight out of ten by boys who reeked of Axe
and sweat, the stench of children turning men.
(It's true, my friends were flawless: lovely lashes
as long as highways, cheap eyeliner pen

we passed from girl to girl, kneecaps like potholes
in ripped-up Abercrombie jeans.) My hair—
"curly" would be a generous descriptor—
was neither "black" nor "white." I wouldn't dare

to call it "ethnic." Even then, I knew
how . . . *wrong* . . . that was, how lazy. So, I reasoned,
some things (or people) can't be labeled. I
craved my own hairstylist who, with ease and

grace, would transform me into a beauty,
a nymph, a supermodel, Halle Berry.
At first, no one would recognize me, gasping
when I walked through the halls. It would be scary

just how breathtaking I had become,
the bullies insignificant and dumb.

Part 2: The Teen Years

I wanted to be anything but what
I was, so I invested in a treasure,
a straightener: expensive, red, and bulky.
Toxic clouds of hairspray for good measure,

too. Each early morning, I would rise
from whatever cruel night terror was killing
me, plug in the lifesaving machine,
and wait to scorch my hair off, now fulfilling

my dream, my duty really, to be hot,
and what else mattered? Certainly not sleep,
or health, or anything resembling sanity.
Did it look great? No, not at all, and deep

inside myself, I knew that. I looked just
like everybody else, though, and for now,
that was enough. I charmed my way through science
courses, wrote long essays. I would vow

to earn all fives on my APs and perfect
grades. I suddenly had suitors. Life
was just how I had wanted it to be,
so why was I so sad? I'd take a knife,

the sharpest in the kitchen, and I'd press
it to my inner wrists, never quite hard
enough to actually bleed. I wasn't certain
that death was what I really wanted. Scarred

by childhood taunts and nicknames, I thought straight
hair would solve it all. Instead, I lost
hours and hours of sleep so I could look
generic. Tell me, please: At what cruel cost

do we conform? I had issues to work
through: father's death, his life, a racial crisis—
you know, the issues everybody has.
I wanted to be drunk like Dionysus,

the god of wine, of fruitfulness, of madness.
No "fresh look" could protect me from the sadness.

Part 3: The Adult Years

When I saw my first therapist, I wore
my hair up in a messy bun. He said
cool things like, "Stop the fighting with your mom.
Your family's down one man already," "Head

to all the parties. Do it. It'll be rad."
Years later, I felt better, though I always
worried I'd get sad again. It'd taken
years to function. I'd pace in the hallways

of my apartment, playing with my hair,
a beautiful, charming collection of
curls with very little frizz, and bangs.
Today, I think I'm starting to find love

with therapists, my hairdresser, myself.
It comes and goes. Some days, I really am
a sad sack. Why is everyone obsessed
with beauty? Is it only me? Goddamn,

it's silly. Still, I do admit I gaze
into the mirror, curls wild but in place.

How to Forget That Night

If anyone asks,
"that night"
never was.
There was
never a night
that was anything
less than moonlit,
dreamy, perfect.
"Those nights"
happen to other
people, not you.
You go months
without whispering
the word, write
poems about cicadas
and jicama. Your
neighbor's dog still
adores you. Romaine
turns tar-black in the
fridge. The TV remains
off. Perhaps nothing has
changed, even when,
some nights, coyotes
howl, sirens offer
sharp-toothed
migraines, and you
epitomize *alive*,
sleeping through the
labor of breathing.
Don't you get it?
Don't you realize
how lucky you are?

Soup Over Salad

In college, I had faith that I'd get better.
I didn't have to write my own obituary.
You might, my therapist shrugged. *But maybe
not.* Life's a gift, they say, but it sure did slay me
when I woke up, made breakfast, lived. Nowadays it's scary

to remember. At the hospital my junior year,
they said I was resilient, typed pages about
my sleep paralysis with the latest med,
a failed science class, how slowly I spoke. Never said
anything too bad, I don't think, how I'd acted out

all those years before: driving stolen cars,
driving my mother to tears. There's quite a bit
missing from that report: my father's words
I never quite could bury, that day at the park, birds
perched in trees above us, watching him spit:

I've never met a child as mean as you. The phrases
that still jog in place today on my once-concrete tongue
when I begged partygoers to call me pretty. I never forgot
screaming at a classmate at a party: *You're absolutely not
out of my league. You just think you are.* I was young;

things were supposed to be easy. Every year, I apologize
to him, to myself. (Diving into the tough stuff—
yes, I have to.) I'm too lazy to fight
anymore. I don't cry daily. Vodka with Redbull doesn't excite
me. Instead, I arrange, rearrange words, more than enough

to keep me from sinking away. In college,
I'd make nachos after the club, burn the spirit out of my hair

with an expensive red straightener. I'd listen to a friend say,
We'll feel better in the springtime, when it's warm. The way
he washed his hands over and over. Today, I am aware

I wasn't suffering alone; others just didn't talk about it. I eat
weekly Thai with my best friend, fantasize about ice skating, text
my mother that life is too much fun to sleep through. I see
my younger self in many others (I won't say who, it would be
pointless, cruel), but I know I'm also different from my oversexed

girlfriends who drive drunk, snort coke in the bathroom at work,
invest in psychic sessions to assure them they'll find love, joy.
I've been called an old soul. I've been called childish. I've been called
a doll, a babe, a talent, a bitch. I don't mind. Sprawled
on the bed alone, I remember (my mouth overstuffed with Chips Ahoy)

all the sadness, anger. Who did it belong to? I've forgotten.
I've heard forgetting is the mind's way of healing. I bet we're stronger
than we think, protect ourselves unknowingly. Life's a golden chain
around our necks of hurting others, being hurt, and back. It'd be insane
to deny that. I sometimes wish I was another girl, for no longer

than an hour or so, just to watch myself laugh, speak, the shape of my eyes,
the way I fidget with my fingernails. The older I get, the more obsessed
with appearances. Once, drunk, a friend confessed she was afraid to lose
the pain. It was all she knew. She made it sound as if she could choose
happiness over misery, like soup over a salad. I was impressed

by her honesty. After not speaking for ages, I saw her
last year at the supermarket. She smiled, but I could tell
she didn't recognize me. I wouldn't either.

Tonsillectomy

With lyrics from Gregory Porter

Before the doctors stole his tonsils,
my brother would silently bob his head
in our blue Jetta while musicians crooned.
The men were middle-aged, jazzy, confident,
with skin the color of toasted walnuts and eyes
like cereal bowls: *fulfill my precious dream*
to bring blues from America to the French African queen!
There were so many reasons to weep.

All week
I have been groggy and ill-tempered. My brother's
tonsils ("biggest ones we've seen!" the doctors said)
sit forgotten like rotting fruit in a sterilized jar
in a hospital hours away from home.
"Finally," he says. "It doesn't hurt anymore.
Finally, I can sing without pain."

When My Best Friend Reminds Me That Nothing Matters

At first, I'm too distracted to respond,
meandering the aisles of Hillside Liquor
while the manager patrols his Ports and Pinots.
Wine bottles, truth be told, are somewhat sexy,
their labels wrapped around like slinky towels,
their posture self-assured. I can't relate:
I've always loved what cannot love me back.

The world isn't my home. It never was.
School shootings, fires, pockets full of loneliness.
Quite a feat at only twenty-four,
my resignation to my solitude.
The world is hardly gratifying, but
the liquor store is. We buy a fat case
of beer, then walk, my best friend in the front,
between the parking spots. A balding man
with donut-eyes (sweet, glazed) smiles over at us,
winks. I hear my best friend's voice inside
my head: *It doesn't matter. Nothing does.*

She's right. None of it matters much, not sonnets;
calories; those rock gods, greasy-haired,
I love. The leather car seat burns my thighs,
but still, I'm happy. Joy's a roll of duct tape
an acquaintance wraps around your ankles, set
to watch you skin your knees against the cement.
I want to cry about this. If I were brave, I would.

On the Appearance of Angels

There are days I want to eat the moon,
to tear it up with coffee-scented teeth,
to flick it with my tongue. Swallow. Choke.
Cough up little incandescent stars. On windy nights
in Baltimore, I wear sweatpants and a crown. I read
stories online: refugee bans, boys-to-women-to-caskets,
Marines share nude photos of female comrades.
As cop cars made of salt speed down my cheeks,
I ask myself if all the world is bad. Maybe not. I once read
about a soldier who met a black man for the first time
after he was shot in Vietnam, his eyes tainted with sweat
and grime, his blood congealing. As the black man
helped him to his feet, the soldier thought,
This, this is what angels must look like.

After

You start to eat again, clip
your nails, sit up straight.
The curtains open, the shower
runs, knots of hair circle
the rust-colored drain. Now what?
No one tells you about this part—
shedding heaviness, a jacket in a sticky
bar, eyeballing the coat rack every half hour,
then every hour, then every two. The awful
pop-song fadeout of condolence. If the bartender
asked, I could tell her how my therapist's eyes went
leaden, hearing of my father, drunk and shoeless
on the elementary school playground. Or about
the epileptic frat guy who said abuse shrinks
the brain. My students watch me as I sit
beneath the classroom's lights, unprotected,
visible, not because I want to be, but because
I have to be. This morning, teaching Auden,
I referred to the stages of grief as "anger, delusion,
and yada yada yada."

Notes to Self

Forget the poetry workshop when a boy told you to stop
using your pain as scenery. Years later, you still don't know
the meaning, though you hear it in the mornings in the mirror,
when you run your hang-nailed fingers down your arms.
You think he'd been wanting to say it since he met you, forming
words the way a painter plans his strokes, pale lips curving into an O,
contorting into sharp-edged shapes. *Stop. Your pain. Scenery.* Now
you've learned pain *is* scenery: encompassing, everywhere.

*

Forget that other boy, this one you dated. He called himself
"a laptop, computing all your beauty and your innocence."
Your first date was at a coffee shop downtown, and you
drank excessively, your mug a crime scene, lipstick blood and all,
his olive eyes too succulent and bright. You two are through,
but in your dreams, you talk over the phone. Your voice begins
to crack when you hear his.

*

Forget that Monday is Migraine Day.
Forget that nearly every day's that day.
Fetal position on the bathroom floor,
remember that *eggplant* in Italian means *crazy apple*.
Remember that your favorite author packed meat for
a living. Remember that you were not born lonely.

*

Someday you'll take a lover on the dusty streets
away from there (wherever *there* is) just you two
and a van, the dirty carpet littered with receipts
and albums. Counting Crows or Wu-Tang Clan?
Your friends, your mother—everyone will want
to know when you're coming home. (Don't tell them.)
Wear golden skin like incandescent sand.

*

Visions leave you restless every night:
insects crawling from a hole in a café wall;

men in uniform dropping to a knee;
your hometown gardeners bent over

their radicchio and tulips, the curves of their backs
ingrained in your brain like a fossil in rock.

*

Do you think Richard Wilbur wasted days
worrying that his poems were getting worse?
a hip professor laughs when you exclaim
your talent's gone. You laugh, too, grab your purse
and offer him some gum, relentless flame
of cinnamon setting your tongue ablaze.
You chew, then spit it out, the wad asleep
inside its wrapper. That same night, you weep
reading your work: *the moon's a bride in white*
oblivious to suffering and plight.

*

This is the last time // you write your feelings // down //

for anyone // to find // to hold against you. A hardcore

embarrassment. A threat. // Look outside // yourself

for once // eat beet salad // hear your mother's voice //

Are you coming home soon? // Come home! // Come home!

Daughters

Sewanee, Tennessee

"We spend too much time writing about sadness,"
Trevor says. He's right. The poet's sadness
is such an irritating trope. I'm glad this

summer, here in Tennessee, I've witnessed
what might be joy snug in my shoes. I've witnessed
what could pass for *healing,* that old hit/miss

word so overused by shrinks and friends
who suffer endlessly, who make fast friends
with chewed-up fingernails, tangled ends

of trendy bobs and updos, far too tired
to keep playing the role. I, too, am tired
when almost-strangers tell me they've admired

my poems for "being honest" about suffering—
good for my art, apparently. *Our suffering
comes from wanting,* an old website, buffering,

informs me Buddha said. But here, right now,
in Tennessee, I hardly want. Right now,
my blood is carbonated bliss, Sprite. How

have I become this overflowing sweetness—
"bubbly," fellow writers call me, sweetness
from wine on tongues, our feelings of completeness

somehow foreign but familiar
at the same time? Mosquitos and familiar
smells of fresh-paved gravel, liquor. We're

those we've feared, those who we never thought
we'd be: the happy ones. I always thought
I wanted daughters nothing like me, not

like whispers in the chaos of the city,
their inky sentences colliding. City
girls obsessed with being "pretty," gritty

and acidic smart-ass words. I still
question everything sometimes: the still
Sewanee ponds, the daily pops of Advil.

But questions lie beneath my cool, gray covers,
total outcasts now. The word *joy* covers
my skin like swelling bug bites. I discover

that happiness is neither strength nor weakness,
the possibility that my own weakness
isn't weakness. Maybe I should speak less

about this so-called angst. It'd be okay
to have daughters like me. I'll be okay,
I realize, frightened, untarnished array

of my worries on a platter, wooden, clean—
relieved, though. Who knows? Maybe now I'm clean,
absolved, a different woman, finally seen.

What Do You Do When the Pain Is Gone?

At a novelty store in Baltimore, my two best friends
make a beeline for the vibrators while I hold band T-shirts

up to my chest: Led Zeppelin, Talking Heads. They giggle,
You're adorable, innocent, like a child. It's funny—I never
thought I'd live to be this old. Years ago, I gazed
out my bedroom window while the sun concaved

like a porcelain dish. I remember a woman in a Jetta
screaming along to Prince, a paper-wrapped churro in her left hand,

cinnamon sand on her chapped, droopy lips. Sometimes I dreamt of her,
thumb-sized, clad in a red flannel nightgown, leaping from the bridge

of her husband's shoulders. I felt blessed to witness it.
Sometimes I miss it, even. Miss what, I'm not sure.

Notes

"Sky, You Don't Get It": the epigraph comes from the poem "The Trip from California" by Kenneth Koch.

"Objet d'Art": the epigraph comes from the song "Sober to Death" by Car Seat Headrest.

"Some Days Are Harder: A Canzone": the quoted line "Shakespeare did adore a twinkling star" references his play *The Two Gentlemen of Verona*, in which Proteus says, "At first I did adore a twinkling star"; the quoted line "It's you that I adore / you'll always be my whore" comes from the song "Ava Adore" by The Smashing Pumpkins.

Dante's modification of a canzone is five twelve-line stanzas with repeated end words, followed by a five-line envoi.

"The Wedding Gown": the final line comes from the poem "Elegy" by Chidiock Tichborne.

"Intimacy": the italicized line in the first couplet comes from the movie *Yeh Jawaani Hai Deewani*.

"On Turning Twenty": the epigraph comes from the poem "September Elegies" by Randall Mann.

"For My Father: A Sonnet Redoublé": the line "It's not your fault" comes from the movie *Good Will Hunting;* "we *must* solve the crisis—in this country —of mental health" is loosely based on a Bernie Sanders tweet from 2020.

"Ted Bundy": the poem is referring to the movie *Extremely Wicked, Shockingly Evil and Vile.*

"Tonsillectomy": the poem quotes the song "French African Queen" by Gregory Porter.

Acknowledgments

Thank you to the editors of the following publications where these poems have appeared (sometimes in different versions).

Able Muse: "Objet d'Art"

Birmingham Poetry Review: "How to Forget That Night"

Cimarron Review: "Intimacy"

The Cortland Review: "Riding Home, Five Years Later" and "Sky, You Don't Get It"

E-verse Radio: "Hoop Earrings, Bare Legs"

Frontier Poetry: "Daughters"

The Hopkins Review: "Luck," "Golden Years," "What Do You Do When the Pain Is Gone?," and "Some Days Are Harder: A Canzone"

Literary Matters: "Seven," "September," and "For My Father: A Sonnet Redoublé"

the minnesota review: "On the Appearance of Angels"

Northwest Review: "Hair Sestina"

Poet Lore: "Ted Bundy"

Sou'wester: "After" and "What Is History?"

Texas Review: "Children of the Streets"

Thanks

Thank you to Quincy R. Lehr, Mike Good, Christine Stroud, Chiquita Babb, and Autumn House Press for making this book a reality. Truthfully, though, I don't know if it will ever feel "real." Every day, I'm in awe of you.

I am forever indebted to the Writing Seminars at Johns Hopkins University: David Yezzi, Greg Williamson, James Arthur, Mary Jo Salter, and Richie Hofmann. You are my heroes. Thank you for making me feel seen, heard, and valued. Thank you for believing in me.

Thank you to the MFA program at University of Wisconsin-Madison for your support and assistance, especially Ron Wallace, Sean Bishop, and Amaud Johnson.

Thank you to Tiana Clark for your generosity and support.

Of course, I owe so much to my radiant, compassionate, and hysterically funny friends, without whom I'd have no material. Isobel Farias, Roshan Berentes, Jacob Lindberg, Stephanie Chou, Peter Vertacnik, Tiffany Eatz, Davide Lucia, Andrea Herron, Chris Sears, Sasha Parkinson, Natalie Staples, Adrienne Chung, Steph Maniaci, and Ryanne Olson: you are my favorite readers.

I am tremendously grateful for the opportunity to attend the Sewanee Writers' Conference and the New York State Summer Writers Institute. I am particularly grateful for Mark Jarman, A. E. Stallings, and Henri Cole. You inspire me more than you realize.

Thank you to my grandmother, Sandra Yoffie, for providing me with the means to pursue my BA in the first place.

And finally, thank you, Mom, for this amazing, amazing life.

About the Donald Justice Poetry Prize

The Donald Justice Poetry Prize falls under the auspice of the Iris N. Spencer Poetry Awards which were created by Kean W. Spencer in honor of his mother, a reader and community servant. The Donald Justice Poetry Prize recognizes the distinguished American poet, teacher, and Pulitzer Prize winner, Donald Justice, one of the finest poets of the late twentieth century. The Justice Prize welcomes unpublished, original book-length collections of poems that pay attention to form for consideration in this competition.

New and Forthcoming Releases

Molly by Kevin Honold * Winner of the 2020 Autumn House Fiction Prize, selected by Dan Chaon

The Gardens of Our Childhoods by John Belk * Winner of the 2021 Rising Writer Prize in Poetry, selected by Matthew Dickman

Myth of Pterygium by Diego Gerard Morrison * Winner of the 2021 Rising Writer Prize in Fiction, selected by Maryse Meijer

Out of Order by Alexis Sears * Winner of the 2021 Donald Justice Poetry Prize, selected by Quincy R. Lehr

Queer Nature: A Poetry Anthology, edited by Michael Walsh

Seed Celestial by Sara R. Burnett * Winner of the 2021 Autumn House Poetry Prize, selected by Eileen Myles

Bittering the Wound by Jacqui Germain * Winner of the 2021 CAAPP Book Prize, selected by Douglas Kearney

The Running Body by Emily Pifer * Winner of the 2021 Autumn House Non-fiction Prize, selected by Steve Almond

Entry Level by Wendy Wimmer * Winner of the 2021 Autumn House Fiction Prize, selected by Deesha Philyaw

For our full catalog please visit: http://www.autumnhouse.org